HANDS-ON JOBS

MECHANICS

KATE ROGERS

Peachtree

PowerKiDS
press.

New York

Published in 2016 by The Rosen Publishing Group, Inc.
29 East 21st Street, New York, NY 10010

First Edition

Editor: Katie Kawa
Book Design: Reann Nye

Photo Credits: Cover, pp. 3–24 (background texture) Toluk/Shutterstock.com; cover Cultura/Tom Lindboe/Cultura Exclusive/Getty Images; pp. 5, 19 (main image) wavebreakmedia/Shutterstock.com; p. 7 Minerva Studio/Shutterstock.com; p. 9 Alinute Silzeviciute/Shutterstock.com; p. 10 Artens/Shutterstock.com; p. 11 AlexKZ/Shutterstock.com; pp. 13 (background), 17 (background) donatas1205/Shutterstock.com; p. 13 (railroad cars) s_oleg/Shutterstock.com; p. 13 (subway cars) MarchCattle/Shutterstock.com; p. 13 (small garden tractor) Konstantin Sutyagin/Shutterstock.com; p. 13 (tank) mariocigic/Shutterstock.com; p. 13 (crane) ivvv1975/Shutterstock.com; p. 13 (mining equipment) abutyrin/Shutterstock.com; p. 13 (large tractors) James R. Martin/Shutterstock.com; p. 15 Christian Lagerek/Shutterstock.com; p. 17 (paper and tools) Garsya/Shutterstock.com; p. 19 (safety glasses) bikeriderlondon/Shutterstock.com; p. 21 michaeljung/Shutterstock.com; p. 22 Andresr/Shutterstock.com.

Cataloging-in-Publication Data

Rogers, Kate.
Mechanics / by Kate Rogers.
p. cm. — (Hands-on jobs)
Includes index.
ISBN 978-1-5081-4367-3 (pbk.)
ISBN 978-1-5081-4368-0 (6-pack)
ISBN 978-1-5081-4369-7 (library binding)
1. Automobile mechanics — Juvenile literature. 2. Automobiles — Maintenance and repair — Vocational guidance — Juvenile literature. 3. Aviation mechanics (Persons) I. Rogers, Kate. II. Title.
TL152.R64 2016
629.28'72'023—d23

Manufactured in the United States of America

CPSIA Compliance Information: Batch #BW16PK: For Further Information contact Rosen Publishing, New York, New York at 1-800-237-9932

CONTENTS

WORKING WITH MACHINES

Do you enjoy working with your hands and fixing machines? Do you like learning about how machines work? If you do, then you might be interested in a career as a mechanic. Mechanics repair, or fix, broken machines, including **vehicles**. They also maintain machines, which means they keep machines running properly.

There are many different kinds of mechanics. Some work only on cars. Others work on buses and trucks. Another kind repairs and maintains big machines used on farms and construction sites. Mechanics also keep airplanes running properly. Read on to find out more about all kinds of mechanics!

DIGGING DEEPER

Certain kinds of automotive, or car, mechanics are also called automotive service technicians. An automotive service technician repairs and maintains the systems in a car controlled by computers and other electronic **equipment**.

Mechanics have an important job. They keep the vehicles we use every day—from cars to airplanes—working properly.

A CAREER WITH CARS

Automotive mechanics are the most common kind of mechanic in the United States. These mechanics focus on repairing and maintaining cars and light trucks. They also **inspect** these vehicles to make sure they're safe to drive.

Automotive mechanics change a car's oil, **rotate** its tires, fix its brakes, and make sure its engine is running properly. These are just some of the many tasks performed, or carried out, every day by automotive mechanics. To perform these tasks, they use many different tools. Some are power tools, such as **welding torches** and jacks. Others are hand tools, such as **wrenches** and pliers.

DIGGING DEEPER

A jack is a tool that lifts something heavy, such as a car. This allows a mechanic to see and fix the underside of a car.

When inspecting a car, automotive mechanics follow a checklist to make sure all the important parts of the car are looked at and tested.

BECOMING AN AUTOMOTIVE MECHANIC

If working with cars sounds fun to you, then you might make a great automotive mechanic. The first step on that career path is to finish high school. If you want to become an automotive mechanic, you should take as many math, **physics**, and computer classes as you can. If your school offers classes in automotive repair, you should take those, too.

After high school, many automotive mechanics go through training programs at a vocational school. This is a school where people learn skilled trades, such as automotive repair.

DIGGING DEEPER

Hands-on training is important for anyone who wants to become a mechanic. Automotive mechanics go through on-the-job training as they work to become more familiar with different tools, tasks, and vehicles. They spend time working with more **experienced** mechanics.

If you know an adult who can fix cars, you can start preparing to be an automotive mechanic now! Ask them to show you different parts of a car and explain how these parts work.

DEALING WITH DIESEL

A different kind of mechanic works on vehicles such as buses, bulldozers, large trucks, and anything else with a diesel engine. A diesel engine is a special engine that runs on a heavy mineral oil called diesel fuel.

Diesel engines aren't the same as the gasoline engines in many vehicles, so diesel mechanics must go through special training to work on these engines. The training needed to be a diesel mechanic often starts in a community college or vocational school. Diesel mechanics also perform basic tasks, such as **adjusting** wheels, checking batteries, and inspecting brakes.

DIGGING DEEPER

Diesel mechanics also repair and maintain commercial boats that run on diesel fuel.

Throughout their career, diesel mechanics are often sent to additional training classes. At these classes, they learn about new equipment and new techniques, or ways to do their job.

MANY OTHER MACHINES

Cars, trucks, and buses aren't the only machines that need repairing and maintaining. Motorcycles and motorboats are some of the vehicles serviced by small engine mechanics.

Another kind of mechanic is called a heavy vehicle and mobile equipment mechanic. This kind of mechanic works on vehicles and machines used on railroads, on farms, and in other industries. Heavy vehicle and mobile equipment mechanics perform general tasks, including cleaning parts, inspecting machines, and repairing engines. They also use computers to check for problems. These mechanics learn their skills the same way other mechanics do—through schooling and on-the-job training.

DIGGING DEEPER

Heavy vehicle and mobile equipment mechanics have to be able to read and understand blueprints. A blueprint is a drawing that shows how something, such as a machine, is made.

WHAT DO HEAVY VEHICLE AND MOBILE EQUIPMENT MECHANICS FIX?

SUBWAY CARS

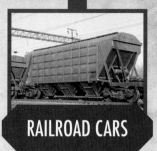

RAILROAD CARS

CRANES

TANKS

LARGE TRACTORS

SMALL GARDEN TRACTORS

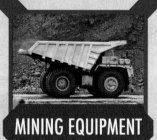

MINING EQUIPMENT

A heavy vehicle and mobile equipment mechanic generally works with one group of machines, such as farm equipment, construction equipment, or railroad cars.

REPAIRING AIRCRAFT

Aircraft—such as airplanes, jets, and helicopters—are very advanced machines. They need mechanics with special skills and training to keep them running properly, which keeps people who fly in them safe. Aircraft mechanics are trained to repair these flying machines.

Aircraft mechanics work on an aircraft's engines, brakes, and landing gear. They also check for cracks on an aircraft's body, tail, and wings. They can check for cracks they can't see using X-rays and magnetic equipment. After working on an aircraft, these mechanics must test the parts to make sure they are working correctly.

DIGGING DEEPER

Aircraft mechanics inspect aircraft according to guidelines set by the Federal Aviation Administration (FAA). The FAA is a government **agency** created to oversee all civilian, or non-military, air travel in the United States.

Aircraft mechanics need to keep detailed records of the work they do to maintain the different parts of an aircraft. The safety of air travelers depends on them doing their job properly.

A&P MECHANICS

The FAA requires all work on aircraft to be done by **certified** mechanics or by other mechanics working under certified mechanics. The FAA certifies mechanics in two areas of work. The first is airframe mechanics (A), which deals with work on the body of an aircraft. The other is power plant mechanics (P), which deals with work on an aircraft's engine. Aircraft mechanics can get certified in one area or both, which would make them an A&P mechanic.

Most aircraft mechanics receive their certification after going to an FAA-approved aviation maintenance technician school. Otherwise, they need at least 18 months of work experience.

DIGGING DEEPER

In order to become a certified aircraft mechanic, a person needs to pass a written test, a practical test, and an oral—or spoken—test.

REQUIREMENTS FOR AIRCRAFT MECHANIC CERTIFICATION

be at least 18 years old

be able to read, write, and speak English

have either 18 months of power plant or airframe training or 30 months of training in both areas combined

OR

complete their education at an FAA-approved aviation maintenance technician school

pass a written test, a practical test, and an oral test

These are the requirements for **FAA** certification for aircraft mechanics if the candidate is a U.S. citizen. If they're not, many other steps must be followed before that person can become certified.

STAYING SAFE

All mechanics—from aircraft mechanics to automotive mechanics—need to be physically strong to do their job. It's a hard job on their body. They often need to lift heavy machines and tools. Mechanics also spend a lot of their time on the floor or in other uncomfortable positions.

Mechanics have a higher chance of getting hurt at work than the average American worker. However, if they follow proper safety practices, they can often avoid getting hurt. Mechanics also wear safety gear depending on the job they're doing. This gear includes gloves and safety glasses.

DIGGING DEEPER

Some mechanics work with **chemicals** that can be harmful if they're not handled properly. These mechanics include aircraft mechanics and automotive mechanics who fix air conditioning systems.

Fixing vehicles can be a dirty job! Mechanics wear coveralls to keep their clothes from getting dirty while they work.

safety glasses

SKILLS FOR SUCCESS

Physical strength is one important quality all mechanics need in order to be successful. Mechanics should also have steady hands because they use their hands to do so many aspects of their job.

If you want to be a mechanic, you should be good at noticing details. Many problems mechanics are asked to fix are caused by things that can be easily missed if the mechanics aren't paying attention to details. You should also learn as much as you can about different engines and other machine parts, as well how those parts work together.

DIGGING DEEPER

Mechanics sometimes need to talk to customers about problems with cars and other vehicles. They need to have good customer service skills, which you can practice by being polite to others and being a good listener.

Mechanics need many special skills to do their job well. They should be good at finding problems and coming up with solutions. This is getting harder to do as machines become more **complex**.

WE NEED MECHANICS!

Machines are all around us. They help us build things and grow crops. They also help us get from one place to another. We need mechanics to keep all these machines working.

Mechanics aren't afraid to get their hands dirty, and they love learning about how machines work. If a career as a mechanic seems like a good fit for you, start preparing now. Ask an adult to show you how to use tools, such as a wrench, to fix things. You can also ask an adult to show you what the parts of a car look like under its hood. That will make you feel like a real mechanic!

GLOSSARY

adjust: To move the parts of a machine to make it work better.

agency: A government department that is responsible for a certain activity or area.

certify: To officially say that someone has met certain standards or requirements.

chemical: Matter that can be mixed with other matter to cause changes.

complex: Having many parts.

equipment: The tools needed for a certain purpose.

experience: The length of time someone has been doing a job.

inspect: To look at something carefully in order to learn more about it or find problems with it.

physics: The branch of science that deals with matter and energy, as well as how the two interact.

rotate: To move or turn in a circle.

vehicle: A machine used to carry people or goods from one place to another.

welding torch: A tool that can be carried and gives off an unusually hot flame that is used to join pieces of metal together.

wrench: A tool consisting of a handle with one end made to hold, twist, or turn an object.

INDEX

WEBSITES

Due to the changing nature of Internet links, PowerKids Press has developed an online list of websites related to the subject of this book. This site is updated regularly. Please use this link to access the list: www.powerkidslinks.com/hoj/mech